ANGER MANAGEMENT ESSENTIALS

ANGER MANAGEMENT ESSENTIALS: UNDERSTANDING ANGER

How do you manage the anger you may sometimes feel at work? Depending on how you express it, anger can have a negative or positive impact on your work. If negatively expressed, it could diminish your productivity and effectiveness, which can also impact your coworkers and the organization. But you can learn to manage anger in ways that will minimize its negative effects and take advantage of anger's potential to provide beneficial outcomes instead.

Factors that are typically part of normal work environments have the potential to cause anger. Common causes of anger include dissatisfaction with the system, unequal treatment, hindered goals, dissimilar values, and hierarchical relationships.

These potential causes of anger coexist in the workplace and are constant. With everyone in your workplace vulnerable to these highly personal, potential sources of anger, anger management can be particularly challenging.

This course will help you understand anger in the workplace by examining how people express anger, pinpointing some common causes of anger, and discussing how to use anger positively in the workplace. After learning about these aspects of anger, you'll be better prepared to manage your anger when you feel it, and then use that anger to bring about positive outcomes whenever possible.

HOW PEOPLE EXPRESS ANGER

After completing this topic, you should be able to match examples of how people typically express anger to the appropriate categories.

1. WHAT IS ANGER?

Physiologically, anger evokes a common response in people. As hormones are released by the adrenal glands, muscles tense, blood pressure increases, heart rate accelerates, and breathing becomes more rapid.

Anger is a natural and basic emotion. It's usually a reaction to a real or perceived threat, and can vary from mild irritation to rage.

Like fear, anger is tied to our instinct for self-preservation. But instead of warning us about potential physical harm, anger helps tell us when our intellectual being, our integrity, or our "self" is under attack. Feeling angry is a good indicator that something is wrong with a situation, circumstance, or relationship.

As a general rule, anger is thought to stem from two emotional states:

- **frustration** when you fail to get what you want, and
- a sense that your feelings are being **disrespected** or **disregarded.**

Reflect

The anger that stems from frustration, disregard, and disrespect is typically provoked by something. Can you think of what some common anger stimuli might be?

Record your thoughts in the space provided.

Write down your response or enter it in a text file in your word-processor application (or in a text editor such as Notepad) and save it to your hard drive for later viewing and for comparison with the alternate opinion that follows.

When you're finished, select the Compare button to learn about common anger stimuli.

Because anger is a very personal emotion, the stimuli tend to be personal too. Common anger stimuli include betrayal, disapproval, deprivation, exploitation, humiliation, manipulation, restriction, and threat.

The stimuli for anger may be external or internal, direct or indirect. For instance, you might find yourself becoming angry with someone who has just disrespected you – a direct and external stimuli. Or perhaps someone says an idea is stupid and even though it's not your idea, you react angrily. This may be a reaction to a past experience, such as being called stupid as a child, and is an example of indirect, internal stimuli.

Anger affects perceptions, interpretations, thinking, and behavior. In fact, angry people are less likely to be able to think rationally. With all these elements of communication adversely impacted, it's easy to see how anger can have damaging effects in the workplace.

Nancy is having a bad day. She's trying to stay positive, but Clarke has just asked her to do one more thing she doesn't have time for. Follow along as Nancy reacts angrily to Clarke's request.

Clarke: Nancy, I was wondering if you could pull the Putnam file for me?
Clarke asks cheerfully.

Nancy: Seriously Clarke, can't you do anything for yourself?
Nancy doesn't try to hide her frustration.

Clarke: Whoa, where did that come from? Sure, I can do it myself.
Clarke's surprise gives way to assertion.

Nancy: Good! I can't do everything around here. *Nancy speaks with disgust.*

Nancy's outburst isn't extreme, but it probably had a negative impact on her relationship with Clarke. Clarke may avoid asking her for help or working with her in the future. This is not a favorable outcome for either individual or the organization.

2. UNDERSTANDING YOUR ANGER

Your organization may discourage the expression of anger, thinking it has no place at work. But the reality is that anger is part of normal work interactions.

Disagreements among coworkers aren't uncommon. Differences in opinion, approaches to work, or understanding can easily lead to disagreement and even anger. But exploring how you express anger can help you deal appropriately with it and avoid the potential negative outcomes of anger.

For instance, do you tend to overreact, letting your emotions direct your actions and possibly igniting the tempers of others? Or do you tend to repress your anger, releasing it in more subtle ways – such as by refusing to participate? Either way, your anger is counterproductive.

Learning to manage your anger will help you avoid expressing your anger in negative or counterproductive ways. You can begin by attempting to understand your anger. Looking at how often you get angry, and how intense your anger is, is a good start.

Question

Start exploring your anger by answering this question. Typically, how often do you get angry while at work?

Options:

1. Not at all

2. Once or twice a week

3. One or two times a day

4. Six to ten times a day

Answer

Option 1: *You are probably a minority in your workplace. Most people do report feeling angry from time to time. Remember, anger in its mildest forms, such as irritation, is still considered anger.*

Option 2: *Experiencing anger once or twice a week is reasonable. You're going to have disagreements and feel angry from time to time. The important thing is that you express it appropriately.*

Option 3: *Depending on the type of work you do and how you manage your anger, feeling anger one or two times a day might be appropriate. Just make sure you're not causing more harm than good.*

Option 4: *Being angry six to ten times a day is problematic. At this frequency, you will definitely affect productivity, and find it difficult to work with others. Serious health implications may also be a concern, depending on how intense your anger is.*

Drawing on the experience of Dr. W. Doyle Gentry – an anger management specialist – feeling angry **not at all, or up to five times a week** is normal and healthy. If you feel angry more than this, you should explore your anger and find ways to reduce your exposure to triggers and learn ways to manage your anger.

Another important component of your anger is how intensely you express anger in the workplace. According to Dr. Gentry, on a scale of one to ten an intensity of six or below is within the normal, healthy range. However, a rating any higher than six is worrisome and is an indicator that you may have a problem with anger. How do you think you rate on the anger intensity scale?

Combine frequency with intensity and you'll gain a more complete understanding of your anger and its potentially negative effects on coworkers, productivity, and effectiveness in the workplace. Being angry can also have serious effects on your physical and mental well being. Leaving your anger unchecked is not a plausible solution professionally or personally.

3. RESPONDING TO ANGRY FEELINGS

Now that you've considered the impact of frequency and intensity on anger, consider how it's managed. Typically, when people feel angry they overexpress it, repress it, or calm it internally.

See each typical way of managing anger to learn more about it.

Overexpress

When anger is **overexpressed** you can clearly see and understand that a person is angry.

They may yell, say hurtful and inappropriate things, become physical, and even violent.

Repress

When anger is **repressed**, you may never know a person is angry. Repressed anger, while

never directly expressed as anger, is generally expressed passive-aggressively.

Repressed anger may manifest as uncooperative behavior, forgetfulness, and missed deadlines.

Sometimes repressed anger may be released in a sudden outburst at an unintended or inappropriate target.

Calm it internally

Some people develop an ability to **calm anger internally** without ever expressing it directly or indirectly. When individuals have learned to manage their anger this way, you won't know they're angry. They also don't retaliate in ways that have destructive effects on coworkers and the workplace.

Question

Overexpressing or repressing your anger can lead to some negative outcomes. And although calming your anger internally doesn't have the negative consequences of these other responses, it doesn't take advantage of the positive outcomes that can come from anger.

Which do you think is a positive outcome of anger?

Options:

1. It helps improve relationships

2. It spurs you to get even

3. It increases your power over others

Answer

Anger can help you improve your relationships with others. It can help you assert your opinion, which is something others will likely respect. However, anger that leads to revenge or is used to threaten or display your power over others will likely have negative consequences.

4. UNDERSTANDING EXPRESSIONS OF ANGER

Anger isn't always a negative thing. Many professionals who study anger believe that if managed and expressed properly, anger can be productive and can even contribute to positive outcomes at work. Positive outcomes may include improved relationships and communication, as well as process improvements and other constructive changes in the workplace.

One anger specialist who believes anger can be positive and productive is licensed clinical social worker Mark Gorkin. Gorkin has developed a model to help explore and explain how anger is expressed. He begins by differentiating between the usefulness and intention behind the expression of anger.

In terms of usefulness, the expression of anger can be constructive or destructive. And in terms of intention, the expression of anger can either be purposeful or spontaneous.

Select each expression associated with usefulness and intention to learn more about what it means for the expression of anger.

Constructive

Anger expression is constructive when it reflects a person's integrity and values while respecting others. Predominantly, this is an objective and rational response to the anger felt.

Destructive

When anger is expressed in a destructive way, it tends to be personalized and exaggerated. It's influenced by a person's vulnerabilities and lacks respect for others.

Purposeful

A purposeful response to anger is an intentional expression. Some thought goes into figuring out how anger will be communicated and what the desired outcome is. This involves significant self-control.

Spontaneous

Spontaneous expression of anger is an immediate response, leaving no time to plan or think about what the reaction might be. Unlike with purposeful expression, self-control is largely absent.

Reflect

In terms of usefulness, is the anger you express constructive or destructive? Is your expression of anger typically spontaneous or purposeful?

Think about how you express anger and write your response in the space provided. When you've finished, select the Next Page button to learn more about the expression of anger.

Write down your response or enter it in a text file in your word-processor application (or in a text editor such as Notepad) and save it to your hard drive for later viewing.

You may express anger differently in different situations – sometimes constructive and purposeful, and other times perhaps more destructive and spontaneous. Returning to Gorkin's model, combining the elements of usefulness and intention yields very different outcomes – some more positive than others. The four combinations are purposeful and constructive, purposeful and destructive, spontaneous and constructive, and spontaneous and destructive.

Gorkin then assigns a single word to describe the expression of anger that results by combining each of the individual expressions. Gorkin uses the word **assertion** to describe anger when **purposeful and constructive** expressions combine.

Assertion describes the expression of anger, where one is mindful of the need for a productive resolution. Self-control helps the person remain calm and rational as she asserts herself – explaining why she's angry and what it will take to resolve the anger. Meanwhile, the values and opinions of others are respected, which increases the likelihood of a constructive resolution. You should always aim to be assertive when expressing your anger at work.

Purposeful and destructive expressions of anger often stem from a person's vulnerabilities. **Hostility** is the word used by Gorkin to describe this combination. Hostility is often a defensive expression, the intention, whether conscious or not, is to attack or retaliate. This response isn't a very useful way of resolving what sparked the anger in the first place.

Hostile anger expression will typically be accompanied by the use of blame, judgment, or guilt-inducing accusations. Passive-aggressive behavior can also be an outlet for this type of anger. Clearly, you should avoid the hostile expression of anger at work.

Question

Match the anger expression types to their associated characteristics. Each expression type may match to more than one characteristic.

Options:

A. Purposeful and constructive B. Purposeful and destructive

Targets:

1. Involves assertion
2. Lacks respect

3. Tends to be personal and exaggerated 4. Seeks resolution

Answer

Assertion is the anger expression achieved when the response to anger is both purposeful and constructive.

Unfortunately, purposeful and destructive responses to anger are disrespectful. The hostility created can make it hard to resolve the anger and garner any productive outcome.

The purposeful and destructive expressions of anger tends to be personal, and exaggerated. This makes positive outcomes to anger difficult, if not impossible.

Resolution is sought in a respectful and mindful manner. Positive and productive outcomes are most likely with this expression combination – purposeful and constructive.

A **spontaneous and constructive** response to anger may be best associated with **passion**. A passionate expression is generally sparked by pure emotion and pain. This is an immediate and unplanned response to anger. Passion is likely to be the result when the anger stimulus touches on something you have strong feelings about, your principles, or your values.

Some self-control is still evident, and feelings and expectations will likely be expressed. However, individuals who express their anger this way may realize they're not in a position to deal with the anger productively, and may request a time-out to collect their thoughts before moving on to resolve the situation. A positive outcome is still possible.

Rage is what you'll witness when the response to anger is **spontaneous and destructive**. Rage is an exaggerated, highly emotional response. It may be rooted in an experience from the past. It's not planned and generally is not useful.

Rage probably best exemplifies the stereotypical expression of anger. You're likely to hear yelling and cursing, and may witness threatening, belligerent, and abusive behavior and even violence.

Rage like this is nonproductive and damaging and should not be tolerated in the workplace.

Question

Match the anger expression types to their associated characteristics. Each expression type may match to more than one characteristic.

Options:

A. Spontaneous and Constructive B. Spontaneous and Destructive

Targets:

1. Sparked by passion and strong feelings
2. An unplanned, exaggerated, often explosive, emotional response 3. Sometimes involves a cool-down period
4. Sometimes used as an excuse to express anger

Answer

A spontaneous and constructive expression of anger is immediate because it's sparked by passion and strong feelings.

Rage is what you get when the expression of anger is spontaneous and destructive. Rage is often unplanned and exaggerated.

Self-control is diminished when the expression of anger is spontaneous and constructive, but typically remains respectful and rational. It may lead to a time-out where resolution is sought later.

The spontaneous and destructive expression of anger results in rage and sometimes anything is used as an excuse for exploding into anger.

Abigail is giving a presentation to a potential client. Things aren't going as smoothly as she'd like. Abigail is distracted because her partner, Mike, was supposed to be here to help with the complex presentation. Not only does she have to do everything herself, she's angry at Mike, which is distracting her from her presentation.

See each of the possible ways Abigail might express her anger when she finds Mike.

Purposeful and constructive

"Mike, where were you? I have to tell you I'm pretty angry that you didn't help with the presentation. I'm afraid the presentation suffered. This is unacceptable. If you can't make a commitment, you at least have to let me know or find a suitable replacement."

By asserting herself Abigail defined her anger and set her expectation for working together in the future.

Purposeful and destructive

"Oh, there you are! It figures I'd find you here doing nothing. I should've known I couldn't trust you to come through for me. I know you'd like nothing better than to see me fail, but it's your career on the line too. I was so angry I blew the presentation, and if we don't get this contract it will be your fault. Happy?"

This is an example of a purposeful and destructive response that seeks retaliation. The blame and accusations won't resolve anything and will likely damage her relationship with Mike.

Spontaneous and constructive

"Mike, I can't believe you let me down. You know how I feel about this partnership. I take our commitment very seriously. We've both put a lot into this. I'm angry right now, so I'm going to go for a walk to clear my head. When I get back I'd like to talk this through."

The passionate response, spontaneous yet still constructive, will allow opportunity for the two to move forward and build a better way to handle these types of situations.

Spontaneous and destructive

"Mike you're such a failure! I don't know why I'm even in business with you. Clearly you have no respect for me and I can't trust you. I can't believe you did this to me, but then again this is just like you – selfish and inconsiderate. Don't forget I can be just as helpful next time you need me."

The response shows rage. It's spontaneous and destructive. In a work environment, this is unacceptable. Abigail has taken Mike's failure to show up personally and crossed the line into disrespect. Mike may not want to work with her again.

Question

Hector has just received an e-mail from his boss that has made him angry. His boss is looking for a report that Hector delegated to someone else to deliver. Hector is about to approach the person, and he's angry.

Given the situation, match each response to the anger expression it describes.

Options:

1. "I am angry because I look like a slacker. Let's figure out a way to keep this from happening again."

2. "Can't you do anything right? I don't know why I ever thought I could rely on you! You're a failure now, and you always will be."

3. "Candice, I have to tell you I'm angry with you right now. I pride myself on being professional and conscientious. What happened? Actually, can we talk about it after I've had some time to collect my thoughts?"

4. "Do you expect me to do everything? You've been determined to sabotage me since I started working here."

Targets:

1. Assertion

2. Hostility

3. Passion

4. Rage

Answer

An assertive response will acknowledge the anger and look for a way to resolve the issue.

Hostility is what you'll experience when the anger response is purposeful and destructive. A lack of respect and tendency to get defensive just makes matters worse.

Passion is the result of a spontaneous and constructive reaction. It lacks some self-control but is generally respectful.

Rage is what you get when the anger response is spontaneous and destructive. It's hard to get a productive outcome from rage.

5. SUMMARY

Anger is a natural, powerful emotion. Learning to recognize and manage anger can help bring about a productive outcome. Aside from keeping employees on task and working cooperatively, anger can bring about improvements to procedures, processes, products, or services. Anger can also be the catalyst for goal attainment.

Everyone experiences and expresses anger differently. However, four anger responses are typical: purposeful and constructive, purposeful and destructive, spontaneous and constructive, and spontaneous and destructive. At work, you should strive to remain respectful and productive. A purposeful and constructive response, expressed as assertion, is best and should be encouraged.

EVALUATE YOUR ANGER

Purpose: Use this follow-on activity to evaluate your workplace anger.

Learning to manage your anger can help you avoid expressing your anger negatively or counterproductively at work. Evaluating your anger by considering how often you get angry and how intense your anger is will help you express your anger positively.

Evaluate the Frequency and Intensity of Your Anger		
	Intensity of 1-6	Intensity of 7-10
Frequency: 0-5 times per week	Normal/Healthy	Worrisome
Frequency: 6 or more times per week	Worrisome	Abnormal/Unhealthy

If you experience anger zero to five times per week at an intensity of six or below, your anger falls within the normal healthy range. Keep doing what you're doing. Of course, reducing this even further would provide further benefits to you and your workplace.

If you experience anger zero to five times per week at an intensity of seven through ten, your anger is worrisome. You should work on reducing the intensity with which you express anger. Your anger will be better received and therefore more positive if you are less intense.

If you experience anger six or more times per week at intensity of six or below, your anger is worrisome. Working to reduce the frequency of your anger will be better for you and your workplace.

If you experience anger six or more times per week at intensity of seven or above, your anger is abnormally high and unhealthy. You probably have an anger problem. You need to work on reducing both the frequency and intensity of your anger.

COMMON CAUSES OF ANGER IN THE WORKPLACE

After completing this topic, you should be able to determine the cause of anger in a given scenario.

1. ACKNOWLEDGING COMMON CAUSES OF ANGER

What makes a person angry in a specific instance may be any combination of causes. But generally, anger is driven by a sense that one's value or self-worth is being threatened. For example, anger can be triggered by feelings of betrayal, humiliation, and exploitation. This points to the importance of respect in all your workplace interactions.

Reflect

What has caused you to get angry at work in the last month?

Enter your answer in the space provided, and then select Next Page to learn more about common causes of anger in the workplace.

Write down your response or enter it in a text file in your word-processor application (or in a text editor such as Notepad) and save it to your hard drive for later viewing.

You might have listed some or all of the five causes of anger that seem to be commonly noted across many different business environments:

- dissatisfaction with the system,
- unequal treatment,
- hindered goals,

- dissimilar values, and
- hierarchical relationships

2. DISSATISFACTION WITH THE SYSTEM

Dissatisfaction with the system is a predominant cause of anger in the workplace. If you find you or your colleagues tend to blame "the system," it's a pretty good indicator that something's wrong with the way things are being done in your organization. Dissatisfaction with the system is hard to resolve; it will take time and dedication to find solutions and defuse the anger that's generated because of it.

In most cases, the source of dissatisfaction with the system is factors that are beyond your control, which then leads to anger. Three typical factors that lead to dissatisfaction with the system are increased

competition, the size of the organization, and higher performance expectations.

See each factor to learn how it contributes to anger in the workplace.

Increased competition

You, and your coworkers, will likely feel as though you have no control over events related to increased competition in the global marketplace. When things like downsizing and outsourcing happen, it can create fear and insecurity, which can lead to anger.

Size of the organization

When you're angry, you need someone to blame. But sometimes organizations are so large that you can't determine who's to blame, making resolution of your anger more difficult.

Bureaucracy and the "one size fits all" policies and procedures that tend to exist in larger organizations can also result in anger. Typically, these policies and procedures don't "fit all," and actually make it difficult for employees to do their jobs efficiently.

Higher performance expectations

In general, employers today have higher performance expectations than ever before. You may feel pressure to be more efficient and productive with fewer resources, while striving for continual improvement.

You may become angry if you feel underappreciated for what you've achieved, or if you feel the expectations of you are unfair given the resources and time you have to work with.

Natalie is a claims specialist for a national insurance agency. Lately, she finds her level of frustration with her job is rising and she's getting angry more and more often.

All claims typically go to a central review board for approval. The problem is that Natalie's clients are often suffering from serious, sometimes terminal, illnesses and need prompt attention. But the review board doesn't prioritize different types of claims, so her clients end up waiting an unacceptable amount of time for claims to be settled.

When Natalie expresses her frustration to her manager, she always gets the same response – "Natalie, you know I can't do anything about this. The national head office controls the review procedure, and they're satisfied that, as a whole, the procedure works."

Natalie's anger stems from dissatisfaction with the system – specifically the size of her organization. The "one size fits all" procedure for settling claims doesn't fit the needs of her particular clients. Having no control over this aspect of her job makes Natalie angry.

Question

Which examples demonstrate the potential for anger caused by dissatisfaction with the system?

Options:

1. With all the recent layoffs, Carla feels she has no control; she's angry, and fears every day at work may be her last

2. John is angry because no matter how hard he works, his boss keeps pushing him to work faster – yet he never compliments John's efforts

3. Freddy's project is slipping further behind schedule every day because someone neglected to get the proper permits; not knowing who's responsible is making Freddy angry

4. Tina is angry because her new laptop has given her nothing but trouble since the IT department issued it to her

5. Walter feels like he's surrounded by incompetence at home, at work, and in public, and it makes him angry

Answer

Option 1: This option is correct. Carla's anger is related to increased competition. Events such as downsizing can make employees angry because they have no control over what happens to them.

Option 2: This option is correct. Continuous emphasis on achieving higher performance can make employees angry if – like John – they don't also receive recognition for what they do achieve.

Option 3: This option is correct. In large organizations, anger can be the result of not knowing who to blame when things go wrong.

Option 4: This option is incorrect. This situation is no doubt frustrating and could create anger, but Tina's anger isn't related to dissatisfaction with the system.

Option 5: *This option is incorrect. It sounds like Walter has an anger problem – he finds fault with everyone. Walter's anger is not caused by dissatisfaction with the system.*

3. UNEQUAL TREATMENT

When was the last time you found yourself comparing your treatment to that of others in your workplace? At one time or another, most people have had these kinds of thoughts: "Why did she get a bonus when I didn't? I work just as hard", "He didn't deserve that promotion", "I just completed a huge project on time and under budget, but I didn't get half the recognition he did", or "I wonder if he makes more money than me."

It's natural to compare yourself to others in the workplace. Often, this comparison is based on a "give- and-get" ratio. You give things like hard work, education, or talent. In return, you get monetary reward, promotions, and recognition. But when you discover inequality between your give-and-get ratio in comparison to others, it may make you angry – especially if a coworker is giving less than you, but getting more. Unequal treatment is another common cause of anger in the workplace.

Question

Fran's angry because Niles always gets to pick his shifts before her and she doesn't understand why. Representatives get first choice of shifts based on performance.

Fran sits beside Niles and knows he's often late for shifts and coming off breaks, whereas Fran is never late for work and rarely late returning after her breaks. Niles has shared his call quality scores, so she knows she has better call quality too. But he always gets to choose his shifts before her.

Do you think Fran is demonstrating anger because of unfair treatment?

Options:

1. Yes

2. No

Answer

Fran is angry because based on her understanding of the situation Niles is getting more while giving less than she is. Perceived unequal treatment is almost certain to cause anger.

In the previous scenario, it was possible for Fran to determine unequal treatment because the criteria for receiving shift premium is defined and communicated to all employees. However, it's wise to remember that normally, these comparisons are based on your perception and not fact. So sometimes it's going to be your perception that's wrong – not your treatment.

Quinton has been working with his present employer for just six months. The company is constantly recruiting for sales positions. He thinks the new hires are being offered better incentives – such as new workstations, better compensation packages, and a higher starting salary – than he was when he was hired, and he's angry about it.

It's important to note that regardless of whether Quinton perceives he's treated unequally or if he really is treated unequally, it can result in anger over unequal treatment.

Question

Which statements are examples of anger caused by a feeling of being treated unequally?

Options:

1. Jill's angry because even though she's been with the company as long as Sandy and does the same job, Sandy got a promotion and Jill didn't

2. Jack is angry because when he was late with his assignment, he got berated, while Kate, who was also late, got offers of support

3. Ross is angry because the standards for certification in his area of expertise will change next year and everyone will have to be recertified

4. Verna is angry because she's heard a rumor that the company won't be increasing salaries during the next annual performance review

Answer

Option 1: *This option is correct. Jill thinks that Sandy is getting a better "give" versus "get" deal than her. Jill's perception of unequal treatment has made her angry.*

Option 2: *This option is correct. Jack is angry because even though he believes he and Kate gave the same thing – a late assignment – they got different treatment in return.*

Option 3: *This option is incorrect. Ross's anger has nothing to do with unequal treatment, since everyone will have to be recertified.*

Option 4: *This option is incorrect. If no one is getting a raise, then Verna is being treated equally, she just doesn't like it.*

4. HINDERED GOALS

Hindered goals are another typical source of anger in the workplace. Achieving goals is typically equated with being successful at work. Performance reviews, salary increases, promotions, respect, and recognition are usually goal related and impact a person's career. When efforts to achieve goals are hindered, it can cause anger because of the potential for it to negatively impact careers.

Goals are likely to be hindered when one person or group's goals differ from those of another person or group. And in larger organizations, this tends to be the norm rather than the exception.

For instance, while working toward long-term organizational goals, the goals of departments and individuals within the organization may differ. However, short-term goals are even more likely to be divergent, and therefore offer even more opportunity for them to be hindered and cause anger.

Suppose a software developer is creating a new program and a competitor appears to be positioning itself to introduce a similar software solution. Management is feeling pressure to beat this competitor to market, or they risk losing valuable market share. As a result, management pressures the software development team to complete the project sooner.

This hinders goals and makes everyone involved angry. The programmers are angry with their team leader because they aren't able to create quality work at a sustainable pace. The team leader is angry with management because her programmers can't work efficiently. As the programmers burn out, quality issues and mistakes are on the rise. This makes management angry at the team leader because he's not getting what he wants – quality and efficiency.

Question

Which statements are examples of anger caused by hindered goals in the workplace?

Options:

1. Ted is angry because even though he frequently reports system limitations that cause delays, action is never taken to improve the system

2. Emily needs to verify employee contact information, but many employees are ignoring requests for verification; it's making her angry

3. Cosmo gets angry when his boss rejects his request for resources that he needs to finish a project on time

4. Kim is furious that George makes more money than she does, even though he's no smarter or better educated

Answer

Option 1: *This option is incorrect. Ted's anger is caused by dissatisfaction with the system. Even though he's reported a productivity issue, nothing is ever done to resolve the issue.*

Option 2: *This option is correct. Emily is angry with her coworkers because they're hindering her goal of verifying employee contact information.*

Option 3: *This option is correct. Cosmo's anger is caused by hindered goals. He won't be able to meet his goal of completing his project on time without the resources his boss refused to approve.*

Option 4: *This option is incorrect. Kim's anger is caused by her belief that she's being treated unequally. She thinks George is getting more than she is, while contributing less.*

5. Dissimilar values

Another cause of workplace anger is dissimilar values. Unlike personal values, which are typically dissimilar, professional values are commonly shared and considered important within work environments. When these values are disrespected or disregarded, it can make people angry.

Reflect

What do you think are some common values that employees might share within a workplace?

Enter your thoughts in the space provided. When you've finished, select the Next Page button to find out more about common workplace values.

Write down your response or enter it in a text file in your word-processor application (or in a text editor such as Notepad) and save it to your hard drive for later viewing.

The most commonly shared workplace values are competency, hard work, and integrity. When these values are shared, employees are likely to be able to work productively and harmoniously. In contrast, when individuals perceive a disregard or violation of these values it can cause anger.

See each value to learn how it applies in the workplace.

Competency

Where competency is concerned, individuals need to believe that coworkers are indeed behaving competently. So, if others are failing to follow known procedures, rules, or expectations, it can cause anger.

Hard work

When individuals perceive that they're working harder than others it can make them angry. As such, when coworkers do things like avoid doing work, take extended breaks and lunches, or regularly leave work early it can make others angry.

Integrity

Integrity in the workplace is about doing the right thing as defined by the industry, professional, or company. As such, when individuals lie or act unethically others are likely to get angry.

Sarah is angry with her coworker Victor. She just got off the phone with a client who was very upset as a result of a previous interaction with Victor.

Last month a customer called to cancel a service, which Victor assured her he had done. So when the customer saw a charge for the remaining annual balance on her current bill, she called to inform the company of its mistake. But, Victor had followed procedure and the plan was canceled. She was paying monthly installments for an annual service, so upon cancellation the unbilled portion of the annual fee came due. But Victor neglected to tell her this.

Sarah's angry because Victor failed to provide the customer with relevant information. And she thinks she knows why – customers tend to get upset when they realize they'll be billed the unpaid balance. Sarah thinks Victor should do his job properly no matter what and that this incident demonstrates his lack of integrity.

Question

Which statements are examples of anger caused by dissimilar values in the workplace?

Options:

1. Kendal is angry because newly instituted precautions will negatively impact his investment targets

2. Kim is working with Holly and is angry because Holly isn't concerned   with

following the approved procedure

3. Joe is angry because Janet routinely takes long lunches and then

he has to help her with her work

4. Lee is angry that he has to manually enter invoices because the shipping and accounting systems aren't connected

Answer

Option 1: *This option is incorrect. Kendal's anger is related to hindered goals and not dissimilar values.*

Option 2: *This option is correct. Holly's lack of concern with following procedure is likely to make Kim angry because it shows disregard for competent work.*

Option 3: *This option is correct. Joe is angry with Janet because as she works less it creates an unfair workload for him – violating the commonly held value that everyone should work hard.*

Option 4: *This option is incorrect. Lee's anger is caused by dissatisfaction with the system not dissimilar values.*

6. HIERARCHICAL RELATIONSHIPS

The final cause of anger in the workplace is the hierarchical work structure that exists in most every business. In hierarchical relationships, each successively higher level has control over the level below. It's quite natural for subordinates to be susceptible to the actions of their superiors – and anger is common in this relationship.

This may be because subordinates don't have full control over their livelihoods – they depend on employers for the means of making a living. Superiors have a lot of control over what and how subordinates do their jobs, which makes many individuals susceptible to fear. Fear combined with a lack of control will often escalate into anger, especially if superiors abuse their power or treat their subordinates with disrespect.

Select each action that superiors might take to learn more about how it can cause anger in hierarchical relationships.

Abuse their power

Those in positions of power or authority over others may feel the need to test or demonstrate that authority by expressing anger. This abuse of power is likely to incite anger among subordinates. On the other hand, when a superior's power or authority is challenged, the superior is likely to get angry.

Treat subordinates with disrespect

Disrespect is a common trigger for anger regardless of who is disrespectful of whom. If superiors treat their subordinates with disrespect, they can expect anger in return. This may, however, be expressed subtly – through unproductive work actions, for example.

COMMON CAUSES
OF ANGER

Purpose: Use this job aid to identify common causes of anger.

Knowledge of what typically makes people angry at work will help you understand your anger, as well as that of your co-workers.

Studies have identified five common causes of workplace anger.

Common Causes of Anger	
Dissatisfaction with the system	Dissatisfaction with the system signals that your organization isn't working as it should and may be causing productivity issues and anger. Three typical factors that lead to dissatisfaction with the system and cause anger are increased competition, the size of the organization, and higher performance expectations.
Unequal treatment	Unequal treatment makes people angry because they think others are getting a better deal in the give and get ratio. This means they believe someone is getting more reward then they are for

	less effort or contribution.
Hindered goals	Hindered goals are a trigger for anger because achieving goals are a measure of success in the workplace.
Dissimilar values	When commonly held work values – such as hard work, competency, and integrity – are treated with disrespect or disregard, it can cause anger.
Hierarchical relationships	Hierarchical work relationships can cause anger, especially if those with power treat subordinates with disrespect or abuse that power.

Consider this example. Dexter, a graphic designer, has recently accepted a job with a small advertising company. He's becoming increasingly frustrated with his job and angry with his boss. Follow along as Dexter explains how he feels.

Why does she keep assigning me such menial tasks? I can do so much more! At this rate, I'll never get any experience and my career will never advance.

And what was that the other day? When she reminded me of my upcoming performance review with a loud laugh? Was it a threat? A warning that I should change my behavior? Or a her way of signaling that I'm getting fired?
Dexter is worried.

Dexter has no control over his career and doesn't like the

direction it's taking under his boss's command. He found her laugh, when mentioning his performance review, alarming and a bit disrespectful. He's also worried and fearful that his boss has something bad to convey during this performance review. The combined effects from his lack of control and fear has resulted in anger directed at his boss.

Question

Match examples of anger to their causes.

Options:

1. Kyle's anger builds as he fights with the supply office to get his requisition approved
2. Liz is angry about Frank's promotion; she feels she's as deserving as he is
3. Heather is angry because her manager keeps denying her requests for management training
4. Philip is rude to customers and has no remorse for his actions; this angers his coworker Claude
5. Tim is angry because his manager keeps assigning him menial tasks

Targets:

1. Dissatisfaction with the system
2. Unequal treatment
3. Hindered goals
4. Dissimilar values
5. Hierarchical relationships

Answer

Dissatisfaction with the system suggests that procedures are not working efficiently.
Liz believes she's being treated unequally. This is a common cause of anger in the workplace.

This example demonstrates anger caused by hindered goals. It seems like Heather's manager doesn't support her goal to build management skills and is hindering her.

Claude is angry because Philip lacks integrity and disrespects his customers. Because Claude's values differ, it's given rise to anger.

Tim's anger demonstrates what can happen when hierarchical rela-

tionships seem, or are, unsupportive and negative.

Question

Beth and Claudia work together for an online social networking company. Both women have similar backgrounds and educations, and they've worked for the company for the same number of years. Claudia has just discovered that Beth gets more vacation time than her and she's angry about it.

What's the cause of Claudia's anger?

Options:

1. Dissatisfaction with the system

2. Unequal treatment

3. Hindered goals

4. Dissimilar values

Answer

Option 1: This option is incorrect. Dissatisfaction with the system is anger caused by organizational factors, such as layoffs or inefficient systems. Claudia's angry because she believes she and Beth are receiving unequal treatment.

Option 2: This is the correct option. Unequal treatment causes anger because people want to be treated equally in the give versus get equation. And Claudia feels Beth is getting more than her without reason.

Option 3: This option is incorrect. Hindered goals can negatively impact success and therefore can cause anger. In this example Claudia's anger is related to her belief that she's receiving unequal treatment.

Option 4: This option is incorrect. Claudia isn't angry because Beth's workplace values differ from hers, she's angry because Beth is receiving more vacation time, which relates to unequal treatment.

7. Summary

The five common causes of workplace anger are dissatisfaction with the system, unequal treatment, hindered goals, dissimilar values, and hierarchical relationships. These causes of anger aren't mutually exclusive - they can work in combination.

Dissatisfaction with the system generally prevents workers from doing their jobs properly and stems from issues beyond their control. Unequal treatment makes people angry because they think others are getting more from the give-and-get ratio.

Hindered goals are a trigger for anger because goals are a measure of success in the workplace. When commonly held work values are treated with disrespect or disregard, dissimilar values can cause anger. Finally, hierarchical work relationships can cause anger, especially if those with power treat subordinates with disrespect or abuse that power.

USING ANGER POSITIVELY IN THE WORKPLACE

After completing this topic, you should be able to recognize how to use anger positively in the workplace.

1. POSITIVE EXPRESSION OF ANGER

The negative effects of anger are generally known. For instance, anger can negatively impact the performance and productivity of individuals, teams, and organizations. Also, anger has many associated health implications, including headaches, stress, and heart disease.

But what about the positive effects of anger? Anger signals when things such as relationships, resources, circumstances, or procedures need improving. Resolving the issues that cause anger can lead to productive action and positive outcomes.

Some individuals learn how to calm their anger internally until the feelings subside without ever being expressed. Learning to calm angry feelings so that expressing them becomes unnecessary is healthier than overexpressing or repressing anger. However, all three ways fail to tap into the potential benefits of anger.

Reflect

Can you think of some benefits of being able to use anger positively?

Type your answer in the space provided, then select the Compare button to compare your thoughts to that of an expert.

Write down your response or enter it in a text file in your word-processor application (or in a text editor such as Notepad) and save it to your hard drive for later viewing and for comparison with the alternate opinion that follows.

Benefits of using anger positively

When anger is expressed positively, the benefits it can provide include enhanced motivation, increased productivity, and improved insight.

You may have identified some or all of the three benefits in your previous response. See each benefit to learn more about it.

Enhanced motivation

Anger can be a great motivator to push you to succeed, especially when you're pursuing challenging or difficult goals.

Increased productivity

Anger can lead to healthy competition, which can increase productivity and quality.

Improved insight

Because anger typically signals that something is wrong, if you pay attention when anger is expressed, you'll gain insight on what needs to be improved and how.

Question

Emma is typically a quiet worker; she keeps to herself most of the time and rarely complains without something positive to add. Sometimes she feels angry, but she never expresses it. She's confided in you that she often falls behind because other team members fail to give her what she needs in time for her to do her own work.

What might you say to Emma to get her to see the benefit of expressing her anger?

Options:

     1. "You're angry because it's not right that this happens all

the time. Use your anger to bring about positive change. Just think of how much more you could accomplish."

2. "If you express your anger, and your coworkers become more conscientious about getting work to you on time, you'll be more productive."

3. "If you express your anger, the insight of your experience may bring about changes that will improve the way work is passed between coworkers."

4. "At least if you express anger to your supervisor, you can redirect the blame off of you and on to your coworkers where it belongs."

Answer

Option 1: *This option is correct. Anger can provide the motivation needed to overcome challenges or difficult goals.*

Option 2: *This option is correct. Increased productivity is a potential positive outcome of expressing anger.*

Option 3: *This option is correct. Emma probably finds it difficult to express her anger, but by expressing herself the information she shares may help to bring about positive change to the process.*

Option 4: *This option is incorrect. This isn't very good advice. Instead you should encourage Emma to express her angry feelings to those who are causing her anger. Approaching her supervisor first may make her coworkers angry too, which won't solve anything.*

2. ACKNOWLEDGING YOUR ANGER

The positive use of anger begins with the positive expression of anger. Four techniques, applied as suitable, will help you express your anger in a more positive and productive way. These techniques are acknowledging your anger, identifying the source of your anger, considering the other person's perspective, and taking action.

Acknowledging you're angry is essential to your ability to make positive use of your anger. People often label their anger as something other than anger. But when they do that, the opportunity to reap the potential benefits of using anger in a positive way is lost.

Question

How good are you at acknowledging you're angry?

Options:

1. Very good

2. OK

3. Not good at all

Answer

Option 1: You probably already recognize the value of being able to admit and recognize your anger. Choosing to use your anger constructively will help you harness its potential to bring about positive outcomes for you, your colleagues, and ultimately, your employer.

Option 2: Being able to admit when you're angry will help you direct your anger to useful purposes. Perhaps you're hesitant to admit you're angry because you've been taught it's unprofessional to do so. The truth is admitting and expressing your anger can be used to bring about positive outcomes in the workplace. Left unchecked, anger can have serious negative implications on productivity in your workplace.

Option 3: *Perhaps you deny your anger or label it as something else – upset, afraid, guilty, and inadequate are typically used to deny anger. Maybe you've learned that anger shouldn't be expressed? Acknowledging your anger allows you to take control of your anger and use it in a positive way – instead of prolonging your anger, feeling tension, or building resentment.*

Amy and Pascal both hold managerial positions and often have to work together on project tasks. Amy hates working with Pascal because she feels incompetent around him.

Follow along as Amy and another colleague, Jessica, discuss how Pascal makes Amy feel.

Jessica: I don't know how you can put up with Pascal's disrespect. I'd be so angry if he treated me like he treats you.

Amy: You're right Jessica, I am angry. All this time, I've been denying my anger by identifying it as my own incompetence.

Jessica: Oh it's not you Amy, and you're not incompetent. It's not healthy to repress your anger. You need to take responsibility for your anger and resolve the issue with Pascal.

Amy: You're right. I deserve respect and Pascal isn't giving me any. Also, the responsible thing to do is work through my anger so I can be more productive.

With Jessica's help Amy has finally stopped mislabeling her anger as incompetence. And she's realized that she has to take responsibility for her anger. Acknowledging her anger will help her better understand her anger and taking responsibility for it will help her take control of her anger.

Whenever you express anger in the workplace, keeping a couple of pointers in mind can help you use your anger positively: remain respectful, focus on what made you angry, not who, and take advantage of the energy that anger provides.

Select each pointer for using your anger positively to learn more.

Remain respectful

You must remain respectful at all times. If you fear you can't control your anger and remain respectful, take a time out to collect yourself. Pursue a resolution to the situation once you've calmed down.

Focus on what, not who

Remember to focus on what made you angry, not who's involved. This will help you when it

comes time to express and explain your anger. It will help you remain professional.

Take advantage of the energy anger provides

When you're angry, the instant hike in adrenaline can make you feel empowered, confident, and competent. This will be especially helpful if you're uncomfortable admitting or expressing your anger – take advantage of the energy anger provides. Of course beware, negative energy can also result in encouraging reckless or destructive behavior.

Question

Which statements are examples of how to acknowledge your anger in a way that supports the positive use of anger?

Options:

1. "The way Terry deflects blame to everyone else has made me angry."

2. "What I've been passing off as fear is actually anger; I need to resolve this so I can stop wasting my energy and potential denying my anger."

3. "Dealing with these constant system malfunctions is frustrating, but I guess I'll just have to learn to be more patient."

4. "Kyle, can you stop yelling at me please? I feel bad enough already, and I can't concentrate when you're yelling."

Answer

Option 1: *This option is correct. Acknowledging your anger to yourself is an important part of using anger positively.*

Option 2: *This option is correct. Often people don't recognize anger but rather mislabel it as something else. Acknowledging your anger is essential if you are going to use anger to bring about positive outcomes at work.*

Option 3: *This option is incorrect. First, you need to acknowledge that you're angry. Making excuses and labeling your anger as something else won't help you make positive use of your anger.*

Option 4: *This option is incorrect. Being yelled at by a coworker would make most people angry. Acknowledging anger is more productive because it offers the opportunity to bring about positive change.*

3. Identifying the source of your anger

The second technique in using anger positively is **identifying the source of your anger**. Be careful not to confuse cause with source. The source of your anger is always you. Realizing the part you play in your anger will help you take control of your anger.

Remember Amy? She just admitted that her coworker Pascal treats her with disrespect and it makes her angry. She hasn't confronted him yet, and before she does she decides to identify the source of her anger. After considering it, Amy believes it's because she isn't being treated with the respect she deserves. So the cause of her anger is Pascal's behavior, but the source of her anger – believing she's disrespected – is directly related to her sense of self. And in this case, Amy's anger is justified.

Once you accept that the source of your anger is you, you may find it easier to explain to someone why you're angry with them. And you need to **take responsibility** for your anger. This means using your anger positively to bring about constructive change – not denying it, repressing it, or over-reacting.

Question

Which statement exemplifies identifying the source of your anger?

Options:

1. "I'm angry about John's promotion because I believe I'm getting less recognition than I deserve"

2. "My coworkers values are reprehensible, no wonder I'm always so angry when I'm at work"

3. "My boss is the reason I'm so angry, and he doesn't even come to talk to me about it, which makes me even angrier"

Answer

Option 1: *This is the correct option. Your anger originates with you. There may be an external event that causes the anger but your response to it is your responsibility.*

Option 2: *This option is incorrect. Your coworkers may cause you to get angry but they aren't the source of your anger – it's your feeling that their values offend you for some reason.*

Option 3: *This option is incorrect. When you understand the source of your anger as something external to you, you will not take responsibility for how you are feeling.*

4. CONSIDERING THE OTHER PERSPECTIVE

Another essential component of using anger positively at work is to **consider the other person's perspective**. Anger is a subjective and typically overpowering emotion, making it hard to think of anything but how your anger is affecting you. This very one-sided perspective isn't particularly helpful or constructive.

So, the next time you find yourself consumed by your anger, widen your understanding to include the other person's perspective and consider why the person behaves as he does. Asking for input directly from the person you're angry with is a great way to understand the other side better. You might say something like "I need to say that what you've just done makes me angry. Can you tell me why you do it?" Be careful not to come across as argumentative by focusing on being clear, direct, and respectful.

Another way to gain perspective is to put yourself in the other person's position, and imagine why he might be behaving as he is. For instance, maybe he doesn't know how to do his job. Or perhaps he's missing critical information, or he's under intense pressure. Or maybe he thinks you're rude and does things on purpose to anger you.

Recall the situation between Amy and Pascal. She often finds herself angry with Pascal because of his disrespectful behavior toward her.

Follow along as Amy thinks about Pascal's point of view.

Maybe his goals are different from mine and he considers me a threat?

Do I represent myself well? Perhaps I'm unintentionally signaling that I don't like him and he's merely reacting to that.

Have I done anything to prompt his behavior? Am I contributing to

this situation somehow that I've overlooked?

Are my expectations for Pascal's behavior unreasonable?

In this situation, Amy is the one who's angry. Asking herself questions about why Pascal might be behaving as he is could help her discover something that will help her use her anger positively.

Question

Which scenarios are examples of how to consider the other person's perspective in order to use anger positively in the workplace?

Options:

1. Frank focuses on how his anger is the result of Gerry's being promoted over him; he thinks Gerry's cold behavior toward him is evidence of his arrogance and that because of this he should not have been promoted.

2. Oliver imagines he's Francine, and realizes that she isn't intentionally acting to make him angry. She was on maternity leave when the new procedure came into effect and has never been informed of the change.

3. Justine reflects on the possible reasons why Cheryl seems to be intentionally trying to make her mad. Justine realizes that maybe Cheryl is overwhelmed and isn't angry – just stressed and a little impatient.

4. Amir is angry with Harold's constant requests for information and decides that Harold is sabotaging him and goes to report Harold's behavior to their manager.

Answer

Option 1: *This option is incorrect. Frank is focusing on his anger and failing to put himself in Gerry's shoes to figure out why he might be cold toward him. This is Frank's perception and needs to be looked at from another perspective.*

Option 2: *This option is correct. Sometimes what seems like intentional behavior to make you mad is really caused by lack of information or misunderstanding.*

Option 3: *This option is correct. Sometimes your expectations may be too high or your understanding may be imperfect. If Cheryl is stressed and overwhelmed, it could be easy to misinterpret haste in her interactions as intentional behavior to make you mad. This is a great example of the subjective, consuming nature of anger.*

Option 4: *This option is incorrect. Amir is supposed to be looking for* *an explanation that will help him express his anger in a positive way. He is focusing too much on his own anger and his perception of Harold. He needs to think about Harold's position to get some perspective.*

5. TAKING ACTION

Taking action is imperative to using anger positively at work. After acknowledging your anger to yourself, identifying the source of your anger, and considering the other person's perspective, it's time to assertively express your anger and communicate the desired outcome. Finally, you can take action to resolve the issue.

In order to communicate the desired outcome, you first need to determine what you want the positive outcome to be. What will it take to resolve your anger? This is the question you need to answer before expressing your anger to the other party. Whatever the desired outcome, you need to articulate it clearly so that when you do express your anger, you'll be properly understood.

Amy has admitted her anger about the way Pascal treats her. She has set her desired outcome – to express her anger in a positive way so Pascal will start treating her with respect. Then, she and Pascal will be able to build a more productive relationship.

When you're ready to express your anger, it's important to be assertive. Simply and clearly inform the person you're angry with that you're angry. A simple "I'm feeling angry right now" is really all that's necessary. You may want to elaborate slightly, "What you just said has made me angry." Or "I don't know about you, but this situation has got me feeling angry."

Remember to avoid arguing. If the person tries to draw you into an argument, say something like "I don't want to argue with you. I just thought you should know I'm feeling angry." Anger is a highly charged emotion and just letting the other person know you're angry can help move you toward resolution.

Once you've expressed your anger, you need to take action to resolve the issue that angered you. What is the desired outcome of expressing your anger? Perhaps you want improvements to make a procedure more productive and efficient. In this case you'd work with the person with authority over the procedure, presumably the person you expressed your anger to, to figure out how to improve the procedure.

Amy, Pascal, and the design team were in a meeting to brainstorm a solution to an identified design flaw. Amy was talking when suddenly, Pascal turned his back to her and asked Roger a question unrelated to what Amy was saying. In this instant, Amy feels angry. When Amy leaves the meeting she goes to find Pascal.

Follow along as Amy tells Pascal how she's feeling.

Amy: Excuse me Pascal, as I was talking in the meeting you started talking to Roger. I think you need to know your disregard for me has made me angry.

Pascal: Come on Amy, aren't you overreacting? I don't treat you any differently than anyone else.

Amy: Pascal, I don't want to argue with you. I wanted you to know that right now I'm feeling angry because you've been disrespectful. I want you to stop disrespecting me. I also want your help to find a solution so this doesn't continue and we can have a more productive relationship.

Pascal: Wow, you're serious. Well, I can stop interrupting you. Would that help?

Amy: Yes, that would help. And can I approach you when I think you've been disrespectful and we can discuss it openly?

Pascal: I can agree to that. That way I can learn how I'm being disrespectful and you don't have to be angry at me. That should make for a more productive relationship in the end.

Amy acted when she was angry, allowing her to take advantage of the adrenaline rush that accompanies anger. Amy articulated her anger and what she wanted assertively. When Pascal tried to argue with her, Amy refrained from getting into an argument with him. Finally, Amy took action to resolve the issue.

Question

Which statements are examples of how to take action in a way that supports the positive use of anger?

Options:

1. "John, your sarcasm isn't helpful and it makes me angry. Could you please stop using sarcasm?"

2. "Joan, now that you understand why I'm angry, can we work together to find a solution?"

3. "My efficiency might improve if you'd stop treating me like I don't know what I'm doing."

4. "I get so angry when I have to work with Taylor, so I'll just avoid her as much as possible."

Answer

Option 1: This option is correct. Assertively expressing your anger is an important part of using anger positively.

Option 2: This option is correct. You need to work with the other person to figure out how to resolve the situation. Asking questions can help you determine what to do.

Option 3: This option is incorrect. You need to be assertive when you express your anger. You're the one who needs to take action.

Option 4: This option is incorrect. It's unrealistic to think you can avoid a coworker because

she makes you angry.

6. SUMMARY

The positive expression of anger can provide benefits such as enhanced motivation, increased productivity, and improved information.

Acknowledging your anger, identifying the source of your anger, considering the other person's perspective, and taking action will help you make positive use of your anger and bring about positive outcomes.

USING ANGER POSITIVELY

Purpose: *Use this job aid to help you use your anger in positive ways.*

When anger is expressed properly it can be used positively in the workplace to bring about positive outcomes. Four techniques can help you make positive use of your anger:

- Acknowledging your anger
- Identifying the source of your anger
- Considering the other person's perspective
- Taking action

Acknowledging Your Anger	
Properly label your anger	Once you admit you're angry and not upset, afraid, guilty, or inadequate, you can take responsibility for your anger and work to resolve it in a positive way.
Remain Respectful	Whatever you do, always remain respectful of other people when expressing and working through your anger.
Focus on what, not who	Focus on what made you angry, not the person who made you angry. This keeps things professional and productive.
Take advantage of	Anger releases adrenaline into your

| anger | bloodstream that can give you a rush of confidence and strength. You should take advantage of this energy to positively use your anger. |

Identifying the Source of Your Anger

| Take responsibility for your anger | The source of your anger is always you. Reflect on your own response to the cause of your anger. Once you identify the source of your anger, you'll be better prepared to take control of and responsibility for your anger. |

Considering the Other Person's Perspective

| Ask for input | Ask the other person why they're behaving as they are. This is a direct and effective way to gain information that you can use. |
| Put yourself in the other person's shoes | Put yourself in the other person's shoes and imagine why he might be behaving as he is. This can help you better understand him and the situation. Maybe you're part of the problem. |

Taking Action

| Communicate the desired outcome | What is your desired outcome? Define what it will take to resolve your anger. Figure this out before expressing your anger to improve your chances of being properly understood. |

Assertively express your anger	It's imperative that you be assertive, when you express your anger. Simply and clearly inform the person that you're angry and why you're angry. Be careful not to get dragged into an argument.
Work together to find a resolution	Ask for the cooperation of the person who has made you angry. When you begin to share the responsibility of resolving an anger-producing problem, the intensity of your anger decreases.

ANGER MANAGEMENT ESSENTIALS: MANAGING AND CONTROLLING ANGER

People have been considering and debating the right way to handle anger for millennia. As long ago as 350 BC, the philosopher Aristotle stated "Those who are not angry at the things they should be angry at are thought to be fools, and so are those who are not angry in the right way, at the right time, or with the right persons."

Virtually everyone experiences anger. But it's important to realize that anger in itself is not a good or bad thing. It's simply a set of physical responses, emotions, and behaviors triggered by a perceived threat or frustration. How people cope with their own anger, and anger in others, makes the difference between anger as a destructive emotion and a constructive emotion.

In this course, you'll discover that anger can be expressed appropriately and dealt with productively. You'll learn about managing and controlling your own anger. You'll also learn how to appropriately and effectively deal with other people's anger, including how to evaluate the issue and provide constructive feedback.

1. Managing Your Own Anger
2. Dealing with an Angry Individual
3. Practice: Responding to an Angry Person

MANAGING YOUR OWN ANGER

After completing this topic, you should be able to recognize examples of steps that can help you manage your own anger.

1. RECOGNIZING YOUR ANGER

The workplace is full of triggers for anger. These triggers include emotional pressure, complex relationships, diverse communication styles, and high-stakes risks and rewards.

Workplace anger is a normal and healthy reaction when circumstances are unjust, personal rights aren't respected, promises are broken, or expectations aren't met. When people work together, conflicts inevitably arise. Different emotional makeups, biases, business styles, expectations, and cultural norms can all trigger angry feelings.

But while many people are adept at recognizing what precipitates anger in coworkers, they often fail to cope with their own triggers. This can result in inappropriate behavior such as outbursts, overreactions, misplaced blame, or excessive self-criticism.

But why should you manage your anger? Isn't it good to just let it out?

Expressing your anger inappropriately can cause you to do and say things that you'll regret. You can cause hurt feelings and engender resentment that can last a long time.

In the long run, this type of venting behavior can tarnish your reputation and professional image. This is why it's important to be aware of your own anger triggers and take steps to manage them.

So even if you consider yourself a calm and rational person, it's vital to have a plan or strategy in place for managing your own anger. If you can learn to manage your anger appropriately, it can be a tool for positive problem-solving and conflict resolution.

2. STEPS FOR MANAGING YOUR ANGER

Anger is one of the most complex feelings that you'll ever experience. Anger has a strong emotional component, but it's more than just an instinctive or conditioned response.

Anger also has an intellectual component. Once a trigger stimulates your anger, the mind interprets the situation and judges the appropriate response. This is why people respond so differently to the same anger triggers. Taking steps to deal with both the emotional and intellectual components of your anger will help you manage it.

Reflect

In your experience, what have you found typically causes a person to react in an angry way? Enter your thoughts in the space provided and select Compare to learn about anger reactions.

Write down your response or enter it in a text file in your word-processor application (or in a text editor such as Notepad) and save it to your hard drive for later viewing and for comparison with the alternate opinion that follows.

The cause of anger reactions

Anger builds up and is triggered through stressors – events, conditions, or situations that cause a physical or psychological response. Once you learn to recognize your stressors, you can make yourself less susceptible and learn to control your reaction to anger.

There are four basic steps that you can take to manage your anger appropriately. The first step is to **make yourself less susceptible** to anger. The second step is recognize how to **calm down** when you start to feel angry. The third step is to **analyze the situation logically**, and the fourth step is to **express your anger appropriately**.

Making yourself less susceptible to anger and calming down are emotional ways of coping with anger. Analyzing the situation logically and expressing your anger appropriately are intellectual coping mechanisms.

3. Emotional response

The first step in managing your anger is to **make yourself less susceptible** to it. It isn't possible to completely avoid stressors or situations that make you angry. But there are things you do have some control over. You can manage your environment, keep a positive outlook, and make sure to take care of yourself.

Reflect

Environmental stressors can have a profound effect on your mood and ability to manage anger. What types of environmental stressors do you think have an effect on someone's mood at work?

Enter your thoughts in the space provided, then select Compare to learn about environmental stressors.

Write down your response or enter it in a text file in your word-processor application (or in a text editor such as Notepad) and save it to your hard drive for later viewing and for comparison with the alternate opinion that follows.

Environmental stressors

Environmental stressors include triggers in the atmosphere in which you work and travel,

pressures from your home life, and issues such as overwork that affect your job performance. These are the types of stressors that can cause nerves to fray and tempers to flare.

It's important to keep a positive outlook. Expecting things to go wrong can turn out to be a self-fulfilling prophecy. The anticipation of something negative happening and making you angry can be a stressor in itself.

Anger is easier to cope with when you take care of yourself. If you don't feel well, you're more likely to succumb to your anger triggers. Even small annoyances can provoke a reaction when you're tired, hungry, stressed, or ill.

See each strategy for making yourself less susceptible to anger for more information.

Manage your environment

The strategy of managing and controlling your environment to reduce anger triggers is called "stimulus control." The idea is that you are in control of minimizing or removing triggers from your environment. Do coworkers constantly disrupt you? Schedule specific times to deal with them. Is noise a problem when you're trying to work at your desk? Invest in a pair of headphones to block the noise or to listen to soothing music.

Keep a positive outlook

Often, a positive outlook leads to a positive outcome. If you anticipate things are going to make you angry, then they probably will. A positive outlook means looking for the good first. If you treat annoying encounters with coworkers like it's the first time something has happened, you can avoid outbursts such as "I told you." It also helps to envision a positive motivation for irritating behavior. For example, think about perfectionist coworkers as caring about their work, not being critical of you.

Take care of yourself

It's important to take care of your emotional and physical health. Eat properly and take time for breakfast and lunch. Make sure you're getting enough sleep and exercise. And don't keep emotions bottled up inside. Stress can lead to illness, which in turn leads to more stress. Expressing your feelings in simple terms to the right people can help diffuse your emotions before they build up to an angry outburst.

The second step in managing your anger is to **calm down**. When you recognize that you're in danger of losing your temper, you can regain control by getting away from the stressful situation, and by using simple calming exercises.

See each strategy to learn more about calming yourself when you feel angry.

Get away from the situation

When you recognize that your anger is in danger of getting out of control, it's time to get away from the situation. If you're dealing with a person, explain that you need to think about things, and will discuss the issue at another time. If you're dealing with stress, take a break and remove yourself from the environment. Take a walk, get a breath of fresh air, or talk to a friend or co-worker who exudes a positive energy.

Use calming exercises

Calming tools are simple to learn and will help you control your anger, rather than letting it control you. Calming exercises can help you let go of your anger enough to get it under control. Exercises can be as simple as taking a walk, visualizing relaxing images, or the tried- and-true method of closing your eyes and counting to ten.

Question

Alexi works as a salesman for a large electronics company.

Which are examples of Alexi making himself less susceptible to anger and calming down?

Options:

1. When a coworker becomes abusive, Alexi excuses himself from the meeting
2. Alexi keeps a positive outlook
3. Alexi makes sure to eat properly and get exercise, even when he's on business trips
4. Alexi makes sure to vent his emotions when a junior sales associate misplaces an order
5. Alexi keeps his emotions to himself when he feels angry
6. When a large sale falls through, Alexi goes for a short walk to clear his thoughts
7. When his stress level starts to build, Alexi closes his eyes and visualizes his vacation destination

Answer

Option 1: This option is correct. Alexi made himself less susceptible to anger by temporarily removing himself from the environment that was triggering his anger.

Option 2: This option is correct. Alexi realized he would be less vulnerable to anger if he kept a positive outlook.

Option 3: This option is correct. Alexi realized keeping healthy and taking care of himself would make him less susceptible to anger.

Option 4: This option is incorrect. Venting anger isn't productive in the long run.

Option 5: This option is incorrect. Alexi will be more susceptible to anger if he keeps his

emotions bottled up inside.

Option 6: This option is correct. Taking a break from a stressful situation will help Alexi calm down, and deal with his anger.

Option 7: *This option is correct. Envisioning relaxing and positive images is a good, simple calming experience.*

4. INTELLECTUAL RESPONSE

The third step in managing your anger is to **analyze the situation logically**. This is an important step toward using intellectual reasoning to manage emotional self-control. Strategies for analyzing the situation logically include using cognitive restructuring, staying away from absolutes, and developing task orientation.

One useful strategy for analyzing anger logically is **cognitive restructuring**. This approach involves examining your ingrained reactions to anger triggers in order to change your behavior.

Because anger is a strong emotional response, reactions can easily escalate into irrational behavior. Rarely has swearing, yelling, crying, or punching a wall ever solved a problem, yet these behaviors can happen with someone whose anger has overtaken rational thought.

In essence, cognitive restructuring uses logic to deal with anger, by intellectually reinterpreting or reframing the stressful situation to produce a more appropriate reaction. This allows you to substitute positive responses for negative ones.

Lee shares an office with Andre. A few months ago, she lost her temper and snapped at Andre because he was distracting her by talking on the phone. Later she felt badly about her behavior, and realized she needed to change.

Now she practices cognitive restructuring – reinterpreting her thinking habits. When she feels upset with Andre, she takes a breath and thinks "Andre did something that makes me angry. Do

I have to respond right away?" Taking that moment to collect her thoughts has become second nature, and now she rarely has to make a conscious effort to respond appropriately.

Another strategy for analyzing the situation logically is to **stay away from absolutes** when you're responding to anger triggers. Absolutes are statements with words like "always" or "never" that imply total fault or place total blame. When you're dealing with another person, using absolutes provokes defensiveness because these statements aren't truths, but products of your own subjective perspective, imagination, and reasoning.

Question

Which are examples of absolute statements?

Options:

1. "You always interrupt me when I'm on the phone."
2. "This computer never works right when I have a deadline to meet."

3. "What can we do to resolve this problem?"

4. "I was upset when you missed the meeting."

Answer

Option 1: *This option is correct. Words like "always" imply blame and can create defensiveness in a coworker.*

Option 2: *This option is correct. Absolutes like the word "never" reflect a subjective, rather than factual, assessment of a situation.*

Option 3: *This option is incorrect. An open-ended question doesn't reflect an absolute statement.*

Option 4: *This option is incorrect. Absolute statements contain words like "always" or "never" that accuse or blame someone or something.*

A final strategy for analyzing the situation logically is to **develop task orientation**. This involves concentrating on what goals need to be accomplished to deal with your anger.

You can define your goals by asking yourself a series of questions to determine what triggered your anger, what the real object of your anger is, and what needs to be done to deal with your anger.

Task orientation means asking yourself the type of questions that help you define your anger and develop a positive goal for managing it:

Who or what triggered my anger?
What are the underlying emotions of my anger, fear, frustration, and hurt? Is there a possibility I may have overreacted?
Am I focusing my anger on the right target?
Is there an alternative explanation for the triggering event?
How can I use my anger in a positive way?

Question

Alexi is feeling angry with Hugh, his company's receptionist. Alexi missed a call from an important customer, because the receptionist left early to go home.

Which are examples of Alexi managing his anger by analyzing the situation logically?

Options:

1. Alexi takes a moment to think about how he'll respond to an anger trigger, rather than lashing out

2. Rather than reacting immediately, Alexi takes the time to ask himself a series of questions about his reaction to the situation, and how it can be resolved

3. Alexi writes a memo to the receptionist expressing his anger that Hugh is never at his desk and is always missing calls

4. Alexi leaves an angry message on the receptionist's voicemail

Answer

Option 1: *This option is correct. Substituting positive thoughts and behavior for negative ones is an example of cognitive restructuring.*

Option 2: *This option is correct. Task orientation involves concentrating on what goals need to be accomplished to deal with the situation that stimulated the anger.*

Option 3: *This option is incorrect. Analyzing the situation logically means staying away from absolute statements such as "always" and "never."*

Option 4: *This option is incorrect. Responding emotionally is tempting, but it won't help resolve the situation.*

The fourth step in managing your anger is to **express your anger appropriately**. You can do this by determining what you want to accomplish, and communicating your anger in the right way. Once you've determined the reason for your anger you can express your feeling appropriately.

The questions that you asked yourself when you were developing task orientation will be the basis for examining your anger and **determining what you want to accomplish**. Of course each situation is different, and so your goal will be different. Perhaps you want to find a way to avoid feeling angry in the future, or maybe you need to confront the person about what's making you angry.

Once you've decided what you want to accomplish, it's time to **communicate your anger in the right way**. This means choosing your words carefully and talking to the right person, at the right time, and in the right place.

When you go to the person, make sure you're clear about what happened to make you angry, how you feel about the situation, what you think needs to be done to resolve the issue, and why it's important that the issue be dealt with.

It's also vital to listen to the other person's point of view. You may glean valuable information that can help you resolve an issue or bring about a compromise.

Project manager Lee finds that expressing anger appropriately helps her to manage when she deals with Neela, a senior manager in Lee's company.

Follow along as Lee meets with Neela.

Lee: Neela, I wanted to talk to you about yesterday. Just as I was leaving the office, you assigned me some last-minute work that was from someone else's project.
Lee is serious.

Neela: Yes, we've all got to pitch in and make sure things get done on time.
Neela is cheery.

Lee: I wanted you to know that I was upset when that happened. You didn't talk to me first, and I felt I was being set up to fail when I was handed an assignment I had no time to do.

Neela: That wasn't my intention. We're all in the same position, Lee. Not enough time and a lot of work. I just needed your help.
Neela is polite.

Lee: I'm glad to help when I can, but in this case I wasn't asked if I had the time to take on a new assignment. It's important we deal with the issue, because I can't do this work and meet my own project deadline.

Lee is serious.

Neela: Well, I want you to do the work, so why don't we meet in my office later. We'll plan a work schedule we're both satisfied with. And in the future, I will check with you when I need your help to make sure there isn't a conflict.

Neela is helpful.

Lee: Thanks. I appreciate that. *Lee is pleased.*

Lee expressed her anger appropriately when she met with Neela. She was calm and polite and listened to Neela's point of view.

When she spoke with Neela, first, she was clear about what happened to make her angry, then she expressed how she felt about the situation. Next, she put forward what she thought needed to be done to resolve the issue, and why it was important that the issue be dealt with.

Of course not all situations can be resolved so that you never feel angry again. Sometimes you can resolve problems immediately, but other times it may be a slow road to progress.

Whatever the underlying cause of anger, and the approach you decide to take, the most important thing is to realize that eventually, you need to let your anger go and move on with your life and career.

WORKING THROUGH YOUR ANGER

Purpose: *Use this job aid to reference the steps for working through your own anger.*

Make yourself less susceptible to anger

- Manage your environment
- Keep a positive outlook
- Take care of yourself

Calm yourself down

- Get away from the situation
- Use mental and physical calming exercises

Analyze the situation logically

- Use cognitive restructuring
- Stay away from absolute statements
- Develop task orientation

Express your anger appropriately

- Decide what you want to accomplish
- Communicate your anger appropriately
- Be calm, respectful, objective, and nonjudgmental
- Listen to the other person's viewpoint

Question

Remember Alexi who missed a call from an important customer?

He determines that his goal will be to help Hugh, the receptionist, understand there are consequences when he leaves work early.

Which are the best examples of Alexi expressing his anger appropriately?

Options:

1. Alexi asks the receptionist to explain to him why he has a habit of leaving work early

2. Alexi meets with Hugh in the conference room, and politely explains that he missed an important call because the receptionist left early

3. Alexi threatens to report the incident to the Human Resources Department

4. Alexi writes a memo to the receptionist outlining his concerns

Answer

Option 1: *This option is correct. Part of expressing your anger appropriately is listening to the other person's point of view.*

Option 2: *This option is correct. Expressing anger appropriately involves communicating your anger in the right way and in the right place. Alexi met the receptionist in a neutral space, and was calm and polite when he explained the issue.*

Option 3: *This option is incorrect. Threats won't help Alexi achieve his goal.*

Option 4: *This option is incorrect. By not dealing directly with the receptionist, Alexi may lose*

valuable information that could help him resolve the issue.

5. Summary

There are four basic steps that you can take to manage your anger appropriately. The first step is to make yourself less susceptible to anger. The second step is recognize how to calm down when you start to feel angry. The third step is to analyze the situation logically, and the fourth step is to express your anger appropriately.

ASSESSING YOUR ANGER

Purpose: *Use this follow-on activity to self-assess your anger.*

Answer the questions and use your answers to self-assess your own anger. If you feel your ability to handle your own anger is having a detrimental effect on your career and relationships, you may wish to see someone in your HR department to find out if there is a program or counselling service your organization can access.

Has anyone at work ever mentioned that you have issues with anger? What were the circumstances?

To what degree do you get angry? Do you ever feel out of control?

Are there particular situations or types of people that make you angry? Why do you think these particular things anger you?

Is your degree of anger influenced by your mood? Do you sometimes become angry over small things, and at other times let larger issues go? Why do you think this happens?

How do you behave when you're angry? Do you repress your anger, or lash out?

Do you think you deal with your anger in a constructive manner? How so?

Do you deal with your anger as it occurs? Or do you let it build until it explodes?

DEALING WITH AN ANGRY INDIVIDUAL

After completing this topic, you should be able to determine which strategies for dealing with an angry individual have been carried out effectively in a given scenario.

1. Benefits of dealing with anger

Dealing effectively with your own emotions can be a challenge, but it's an important part of developing empathy. Using empathy – the ability to understand how other people feel – is a productive starting point for dealing with anger in other people.

Reflect

Think of a time when you were angry and someone tried to manage your anger. How did that make you feel?

Enter your thoughts in the space provided and select Next Page to learn about empathy.

Write down your response or enter it in a text file in your word-processor application (or in a text editor such as Notepad) and save it to your hard drive for later viewing.

You may have recalled a time when someone helped deal with your anger. Or perhaps you thought of a situation where someone's behavior made you even more angry. Remembering what it felt like when you were angry, and how you reacted when another person engaged with you, helps you to understand how other people might feel when you try to manage their anger. This is known as empathy.

When you're able to empathize with angry subordinates, superiors, or peers, you'll benefit by promoting change in how those people behave toward you in the future. You'll also define the boundaries of your relationships by letting people know appropriate ways of behaving toward you.

See each benefit of effectively dealing with angry individuals for more information.

Promote behavior change

Dealing effectively with an angry individual promotes change in how that person behaves around you in future interactions. Put simply, it will help you build a positive relationship, which will help the angry person understand what type of behavior will garner positive results.

Define boundaries of relationships

Personal boundaries are rules or limits that define reasonable and permissible ways for other people to behave around you. It's vital to be consistent with your responses when someone steps outside those limits, and to respect the other person's boundaries. This helps you define the limits of future interactions with the angry individual.

Question

What are the benefits of dealing effectively with angry individuals?

Options:

1. It will help change their behavior for the better
2. It will allow you to define the boundaries of your future interactions with them 3. It will allow you to deal with all types of angry individuals
4. It will prevent coworkers from ever becoming angry with you

again

Answer

Option 1: *This option is correct. When you promote behavioral change for angry individuals, you help them understand what type of behavior will garner positive results in the future.*

Option 2: *This option is correct. Defining boundaries in your relationships will set limits in future interactions with angry individuals.*

Option 3: *This option is incorrect. It's not always your responsibility to get involved in other people's anger.*

Option 4: *This option is incorrect. You can't prevent other people from getting angry, but dealing effectively with anger can help promote change in how that person behaves around you in the future.*

2. Strategies for dealing with anger

Dealing inappropriately with another person's anger can often make a situation worse. The other person may become even angrier, or may conclude that getting angry is the appropriate way to deal with you.

There are three common ineffective ways that some use to cope with angry people. These are ignoring the anger, shutting down the angry person, and competing with the other person's anger.

See each ineffective coping behavior for more information about dealing with anger.

Ignoring

It's uncomfortable to deal with an angry person, but ignoring the anger won't make the problem go away. Acknowledging that a person is angry is the first step to dealing with the situation.

Shutting them down

People that are angry often feel the need to express their emotions. Shutting them down through nonverbal communication such as "shushing" is disrespectful and sends the message that their feelings aren't legitimate.

Competing

Meeting anger with more anger only serves to exacerbate the situation. If you attempt to compete by shouting down at an angry individual, or otherwise overreact, the situation can spiral out of control. It may even lead to a physical confrontation.

There are four main strategies that can help you manage when you're in a situation where you have to deal with someone's anger. You'll need to manage your own anger first, identify the underlying source of the anger, assert yourself verbally, and provide the person with feedback.

3. MANAGE YOUR OWN ANGER

The first strategy is to **manage your own anger**. Appropriately managing an angry person starts with being aware of your own feelings of anger, and recognizing what your own triggers are.

It's easier to deal with an angry individual when you're aware of your own feelings. Recalling what it feels like when you're angry creates self-awareness and allows you to empathize with the other person.

Self-awareness also involves recognizing your own anger triggers. If you're aware that whining or being shouted at are triggers that make you angry, you can mentally prepare for them. It also helps to anticipate and practice how to deal with your triggers.

Zach is a new manager at a software company. Follow along as he deals with Jen, an angry direct report.

Jen: I need to talk to you right now. I'm really upset.

Zach: Jen, I'm in a rush. Whatever it is, just deal with it, OK?

Jen: I'm in a hurry too. And no one will be happy if we miss this project deadline. You really have to do something about Doug. I can't get my work done without his reports, and they're late, again!

Zach: Shush. Keep your voice down.

Jen: This isn't my fault. I am trying to keep things on schedule, and Doug's just being stupid about it.

Zach: Don't use that word. You know it irritates me.

Jen: Well, excuse me for caring about my work. Next time, I'll just do my own work, and to heck with the deadlines.

Zach didn't deal appropriately with Jen because he wasn't able to manage his own anger. If he had been more empathetic to Jen's feelings, he would have realized that she was concerned with meeting her deadline. And if he was more in tune with his own anger triggers, he wouldn't have lost his temper when Jen used a word he didn't like. If Zach had done a better job of managing his own anger, he would have been better able to cope with Jen's emotions, and preserved her sense of teamwork.

4. IDENTIFY THE SOURCE

The second strategy in managing anger is to **identify the source of the anger**. This involves gathering information about the issue, setting up a meeting, and conducting the meeting appropriately.

See each step toward identifying the underlying source for more information.

Gather information

When someone is angry, there's usually a reason for it. But it's important to be objective. If you only listen to one side of the issue, you won't get a clear picture of the situation. You need to talk to other people to find out why the person is angry, what happened to precipitate the issue, and whether there are any extenuating circumstances. For example, are there personal issues that are influencing work performance? Is the issue part of a long-running feud?

Set up a meeting

It's important to deal with a person's anger, but it doesn't have to happen immediately. Setting up a meeting for later in the day will acknowledge the issue, but also give the angry individual some time to calm down. Select a time and place that is comfortable for both of you. But don't leave it too long, or you risk the anger building again.

Conduct the meeting appropriately

When you do meet with the angry individual, you need to conduct the meeting appropriately. This means listening to what's being said, staying with the core issue, and moving toward a resolution of that issue. Remember that empathetic responses diffuse negative emotions. Responding appropriately will create a more congenial problem-solving atmosphere.

When you meet with people who are angry, they may not always see an issue in the same way that you do. This is particularly true if the anger is directed toward you. To successfully resolve the issue, it's important to listen to the other side of the story. Let the angry person have a say, and then reflect back on what was said without judgment. If the anger starts to escalate, or the person is repeating points or speaking in absolutes, it's time to gently and respectively cut off that part of the conversation, and state your response.

After you've had your turn to speak, find the points that you both agree on, and work toward a resolution.

As part of his management training at the software company, Zach has been working on his anger management skills. He is aware his direct report Jen is upset again about the poor time-management skills of Doug, one of her teammates. Zach has arranged a meeting with Jen to discuss the issue. Prior to the meeting, Zach discusses the issue with the rest of the team members, and also reviews the time lines for their last several projects.

Follow along as Zach meets with Jen in the boardroom, and deals with her anger.

Zach: Thanks for agreeing to meet with me, Jen. Now, tell me the issue as you see it. I'm here to listen to you.

Jen: I'm so angry. I can't work with Doug anymore. He hands off work to me late. Then I get blamed, or have to work overtime to meet my deadlines.

Zach: So you're angry with Doug because he missed deadlines that affected your own work.

Jen: Yes. He's late every single time.

Zach: Well, I checked the past few projects, and it seems Doug has been late twice before the last time.

Jen: Well, OK. But that's still three times.

Zach: So we agree that Doug's been late three times, and that you're angry because it's adversely affecting your own work. I want you to know I'm going to speak with him and do my best to resolve the situation.

In this case, Zach did well in dealing with the source of Jen's anger. He gathered information about the issue by speaking with team members. He met with Jen in a neutral location and listened to her complaint. He used the information he had gathered to respectfully counter Jen's absolute statement that Doug was always late. He also stated the points he and Jen agreed on, and stayed with the core issue by restating and acknowledging Jen's concerns.

Question

Nita is a manager at a graphic design company. Recently she overheard Paul, one of her new direct reports, yelling at a colleague.

Which of the strategies for dealing with an angry individual has Nita carried out effectively here?

Options:

1. Nita speaks to the colleague that Paul was angry at to find out what precipitated the issue
2. Nita asks Paul to meet with her later in the day
3. Nita takes time to prepare for the meeting by remembering what it was like to be a new employee
4. Nita immediately requests that Paul be quiet and leave the room

5. Nita makes a conscious effort to remain calm even though Paul's behavior irritates her

6. Nita decides to let Paul work out the situation on his own

Answer

Option 1: *This option is correct. Gathering information about the anger issue is part of identifying the source of Paul's anger.*

Option 2: *This option is correct. Meeting with Paul is part of identifying the source of his anger. Setting up a meeting for later in the day acknowledges Paul's anger issue, but also gives him some time to calm down.*

Option 3: *This option is correct. Empathy is a part of the strategy of managing your own anger.*

Option 4: *This option is incorrect. Nita should gather information about the anger issue before she decides that Paul is at fault.*

Option 5: *This option is correct. Understanding your triggers is part of the strategy of managing your own anger.*

Option 6: *This option is incorrect. As a manager, Nita has a responsibility to deal with the situation.*

5. ASSERT YOURSELF

The third strategy in managing anger is to **assert yourself verbally**. When people are angry, emotions run high. Sometimes, this means that angry people resort to unacceptable behavior. This can include personal attacks, verbal putdowns, and threats. In these cases, it's important to be calm and assertive.

If negative behavior persists in the meeting, explain your concerns and try to get the meeting back on track. Remember that you shouldn't have to endure abuse. If you feel threatened or uncomfortable with someone's behavior, state the problem. You could suggest taking a break or rescheduling the meeting. If the negative behavior continues or escalates, ask the person to leave, or leave yourself.

Doug has encountered his manager, Zach, in the staff room of the software company where they work. Follow along as Zach deals with Doug's negative behavior.

Doug: I've been looking for you. What's going on? Why are you telling other people I'm doing lousy work?

Zach: No, Doug. That's not what this is about. I was just speaking with Jen about her work. You know her timelines are dependent on yours.

Doug: Oh, yes. You and Jen. That's cozy.

Zach: Come and meet with me later this afternoon. We'll talk about the timeline issue then.

Doug: You've got your favorites and that's it. I work hard and I don't get acknowledged. No one gives me a break in this ridiculous place.

Zach: Doug, I understand you're angry, but that's not appropriate behavior. I'm going back to my office now. I'll speak with you later today, when you've had a chance to think about this.

Zach handled the situation with Doug in an appropriate manner. First he tried to steer Doug back on track. Then, he suggested that Doug meet with him at a later time. When Doug's behavior worsened, Zach stated his intentions and left the volatile situation.

6. Evaluate and provide feedback

The fourth strategy in managing anger is to **evaluate the issue and provide constructive feedback** to the angry individual. This involves evaluating if the anger was legitimate, providing feedback, and seeking a solution to the issue.

After you've listened to the angry person's side of the story, you'll need to evaluate whether the anger is legitimate, and whether the behavior is appropriate to the situation. It may help to inquire whether there is something in the work environment that is causing anxiety.

Once you've evaluated the anger, it's time to provide constructive feedback. Your goal should be to help people get over the anger and improve performance, not to demoralize them.

There are three points to cover when you're providing constructive feedback. You need to describe the person's behavior, state your expectations about how you want to be treated, and seek a solution to the issue.

See each feedback point for more information.

Describe the behavior

The first point of providing feedback is to give a straightforward description of the behavior you observed and want to discourage. It's important to remain unbiased, and not to impart blame.

State expectations

The next point is to state your expectations of how you expect to be treated in the future. This doesn't involve judging whether people are right or wrong in feeling angry. It's about letting them know how you expect them to exhibit anger in their interactions with you. This is a good time to discuss the appropriateness of the behavior in terms of its workplace impact.

Seek a solution

Your final point of providing feedback should be to seek a solution to the anger issue. If the issue was your fault, suggest a proactive way the angry person can handle the situation in the future. If you're a manager dealing with a direct report, lay out a clear description of the expected new behavior. Before you conclude your meeting, it's important to state the points that you and the other person have agreed upon – how he or she should behave in future, and how you can help in this regard.

Zach has arranged to meet with Doug to deal with Doug's anger issue. To prepare, Zach has discussed the issue with Doug's teammates. Follow along as Zach evaluates the issue and provides Doug with feedback.

Zach: You were angry earlier today. I'd like to help, even if you are upset with me. Now, do you really think I play favorites? Or is there something else on your mind?
Zach is concerned.

Doug: I'm sorry I said that. I was just upset because Jen is blaming me for making the project late. I'm in the same situation she is. If I get my work late, then I'm late handing it off to her.
Doug is annoyed.

Zach: Would it be fair to say that you have a reason for being upset, but you've overreacted and focused your anger in the wrong direction?

Zach is helpful.

Doug: Jen shouldn't blame me. The real problem is that the work is delayed earlier in the process.
Doug is upset.

Zach: I understand what you're saying. Now Doug, I want to say that I value our work relationship, but I have some concerns I need to discuss with you. Your expression of anger this morning wasn't appropriate for the workplace.

Zach is concerned.

Doug: I was just at the breaking point. Jen was blaming me, and then you showed up and I just saw red.
Doug is apologetic.

Zach: I'm going to work with you to get the time line issue straightened out. In the future, if you're angry, make an appointment and come talk with me before you reach a crisis point. And make an effort to talk to Jen and tell her ahead of time if work is going to be late.

Zach is helpful.

Zach handled the issue of Doug's anger in an appropriate manner by evaluating the issue, and providing constructive feedback. Understanding the source of Doug's anger – frustration with his time lines – Zach was able to evaluate the legitimacy of the anger, and offered to work with Doug on a solution to the issue and to Doug's anger.

Question

Nita is meeting with Paul to discuss his angry outburst earlier in the day.

Which strategies for dealing with an angry individual does Nita carry out effectively?

Options:

1. When Paul begins to get agitated during the meeting, Nita suggests they take a short break

2. Nita asks Paul to tell her what he was angry about, and listens carefully to his story

3. Nita explains to Paul that she expects him to deal with colleagues in a calm manner from this point on

4. 4. Nita asks Paul to sit quietly while she outlines her expectations for his behavior 5. Nita tells Paul that she'll issue a formal reprimand if the behavior continues

Answer

Option 1: *This option is correct. Taking a break when Paul's anger starts to escalate is part of the strategy of Nita asserting herself verbally.*

Option 2: *This option is correct. Letting the angry person tell their side of the story is part of evaluating the issue.*

Option 3: *This option is correct. Providing feedback includes laying out a description of the expected new behavior.*

Option 4: *This option is incorrect. Evaluating the issue and providing feedback includes interacting with the individuals and letting them tell their side of the story.*

Option 5: *This option is incorrect. The purpose of feedback is to improve Paul's performance, not to demoralize him.*

7. SUMMARY

There are four main strategies that can help you manage when you're dealing with someone's anger in the workplace. The strategies are to manage your own anger, identify the underlying source of the individual's anger, assert yourself verbally if negative behavior continues, and evaluate the issue and provide constructive feedback to the angry individual.

DEALING WITH ANGER IN OTHERS

Purpose: *Use this job aid to reference strategies for dealing with another person's anger.*

There are four main strategies that can help you manage when you're in a situation where you have to deal with someone's anger.

1. Manage your own anger

   - Be aware of your feelings
   - Recognize your own anger triggers

2. Identify the underlying source of the anger

   - Gather information about the anger issue
   - Set up a meeting to discuss the issue
   - Conduct the meeting appropriately

     - Listen to what is being said
     - Keep the meeting on track
     - Move toward a resolution of the issue

3. Assert yourself verbally

   - If negative behavior persists in the meeting, explain your concerns and try to get the meeting back on track.
   - If you feel threatened or uncomfortable, state the problem, and ask the person to leave or leave yourself.

4. Evaluate the issue and provide constructive feedback

- Evaluate if the anger was legitimate
- Provide feedback
- Seek a solution to the issue